IMAGES
of America

ROCHESTER'S
TRANSPORTATION HERITAGE

MAP OF TROLLEY AND INTERURBAN LINES 1910-1920

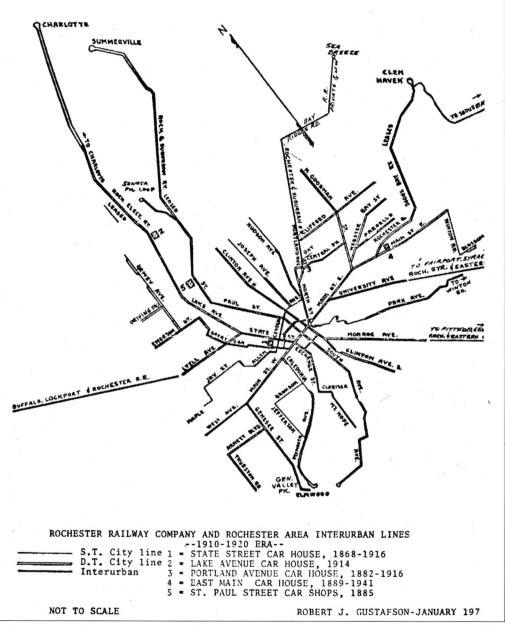

ROCHESTER RAILWAY COMPANY AND ROCHESTER AREA INTERURBAN LINES
--1910-1920 ERA--

———— S.T. City line	1 =	STATE STREET CAR HOUSE, 1868-1916
═══════ D.T. City line	2 =	LAKE AVENUE CAR HOUSE, 1914
━━━━ Interurban	3 =	PORTLAND AVENUE CAR HOUSE, 1882-1916
	4 =	EAST MAIN CAR HOUSE, 1889-1941
	5 =	ST. PAUL STREET CAR SHOPS, 1885

NOT TO SCALE

ROBERT J. GUSTAFSON-JANUARY 197

Like a spider web, the tracks for Rochester's trolley lines spread out through the center of the city. Three interurban lines took riders to other cities, and four lines went to amusement parks.

IMAGES
of America

ROCHESTER'S
TRANSPORTATION HERITAGE

Donovan A. Shilling

ARCADIA

Published by Arcadia Publishing,
an imprint of Tempus Publishing Inc.
2A Cumberland Street
Charleston, SC 29401

Printed in Great Britain.

Library of Congress Catalog Card Number:2003108611

For all general information, contact Arcadia Publishing:
Telephone 843-853-2070
Fax 843-853-0044
E-mail sales@arcadiapublishing.com

For customer service and orders:
Toll-free 1-888-313-2665

Visit us on the Internet at www.arcadiapublishing.com.

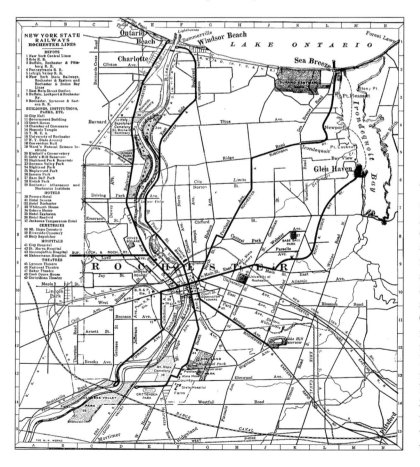

The c. 1912 map is an outstanding graphic, finely detailing both the streets and the nine rail lines that served Rochester. Shown on the map are the Erie Canal's route, the rail and interurban routes, and locations mentioned in the book. Norton Street was part of the city limits when this map was created.

CONTENTS

ACKNOWLEDGMENTS

The writer is most grateful for the support and encouragement of the members of the New Society of the Genesee. The members of the New York Museum of Transportation and the Rochester chapter of the National Railway Historical Society (NRHS) also deserve my gratitude for permission to use their photographs. Many of the rare images of the past came from Jim Feasel and John Ignizzio. My special thanks to Gerry Muhl, Jim Dierks, and my wife, Yolanda, for their advice and review of the manuscript.

This book is dedicated to all those friends and acquaintances who are working through historic research or hands-on projects to preserve Rochester's transportation heritage.

INTRODUCTION

An essential component of any prosperous region is the ability for its citizens to employ transportation systems that move them to places of labor and leisure in a timely manner, and to facilitate the swift movement of goods within the community, as well as to and from more distant geographic areas. Rochester has a long and colorful series of transportation modes, including watercraft and aircraft, horses and iron horses, and even a subway system.

From its days as the hamlet called Rochesterville in 1812, when it was served by sailing sloops and later by lake steamers, to its days as Monroe County's great metropolis, served by turbine-driven airplanes in the 1950s, the city has experienced a number of transportation developments. These changes are illustrated in scores of lively, rare, and unusual photographs within *Rochester's Transportation Heritage*.

Recapture those bygone days by viewing scenes of the grand Erie Canal and by perusing photographs of old dobbin as a workhorse as well as a racehorse. As times changed, horse cars were replaced by swifter conveyances. Imagine the rolling thunder of the magnificent trolley and interurban cars, propelled by electricity, gliding over the miles of iron rails installed in the city streets. Included here is a unique photograph of the rotary snowplow invented by Charles Ruggles in Charlotte to remove snowdrifts from trolley tracks.

Vintage images of the downtown's streets reveal its busy traffic and the work continually performed to improve travel for the populace. With this, the great bicycle craze is noted through pictures of bicycle or "wheel" clubs, with girls wearing bloomers and men wearing knickers. One will discover an illustration of the famous Elsa Von Blumen, who raced her bicycle against a trotting mare at Rochester's driving park.

The construction of railroads to and from Rochester transformed the city from a leisurely canal port into a bustling railway center. A full chapter documents Rochester's railroads and their rail stations, particularly Claude Bragdon's masterpiece, the handsome New York Central Station at Clinton and Central Avenues.

The era that saw horses give way to horseless carriages is represented by vivid photographs of automobiles, trucks, and buses. Two images are especially interesting. One reveals a nearly unknown Rochester-made automobile called the Regas. The other is an advertisement placed by George B. Selden in the January 1904 issue of *Scientific American*. As the inventor of the nation's first vehicle driven by an internal combustion engine in 1877, he warned that he would sue all those who have infringed on his patents.

The airplane, the latest mode of transportation, is documented. Early aerial flights over Rochester are depicted, as well as the expansion of the municipal airport into Rochester's

Monroe County Airport. One photograph records Charles Lindbergh's visit to the city.

The final chapter is a tribute to those who share the author's strong belief in preserving the best of yesterday's travel modes to ensure that generations both today and tomorrow may appreciate Rochester's rich transportation heritage. To this end, the New York Museum of Transportation has joined with the Rochester chapter of the National Railway Historical Society. Its members have actively pursued a comprehensive program to acquire, restore, and operate examples of the historic vehicles once used in the region. Scheduled presentations are provided for the public's interest and education. The two organizations offer trolley, track car, and train rides, plus displays of automobiles, carriages, trolleys, buses, a period fire engine, and vintage construction equipment.

This 1934 photograph seems appropriate for use in a photographic history of Rochester's transportation heritage. In the center is Broad Street, once the largest aqueduct on the Erie Canal. Tracks circling right from below the road are part of the subway, seen prior to the building of the main library. On the right, Court Street carries traffic over the Genesee River. Adjacent to Court Street, in the upper right, is the Lehigh Valley Railroad station. The Genesee River, another avenue of transportation for the city, flows through the center of the photograph.

One
THE ERIE CANAL AND
ONTARIO LAKE BOATS

This *c.* 1909 photograph was taken from the east bank of the Genesee River. On the right, members of the Rochester Sailing Club gather on the dock during one of their summer social gatherings and clambakes. A lake steamer is heading upriver on the left. Charlotte and the Ontario Beach Amusement Park are seen across the river.

The Genesee River served as a scenic gateway into Rochester for many years. Capt. J.D. Scott appears with his boat, the *City of Rochester*, arriving at the Old Steamboat Landing. The steamer allowed diners and vacationers to reach the Glen House on the Genesee River's edge just north of the Genesee's lower falls. Captain Scott's steamer carried passengers between the Glen House and the port of Charlotte on regularly scheduled trips.

The *Titania* was one of the vessels used by Capt. J.D. Scott ("the Excursion King"), who promoted river, lake, and bay-side picnics and outings. A 50¢ round-trip ticket took one by streetcar from Main Street to Charlotte, then by lake steamer to Sea Breeze, for stops at resorts on Irondequoit Bay by naphtha launch. Another trolley returned passengers to downtown. What a day's ride for 50¢.

To Sunday School

PLEASURE ❧ PARTIES.

J. D. SCOTT will furnish Lowest Rates for transportation by Railroads, Steamers and Street Cars. Address him by letter at No. 5 Powers Block, and he will call and see you.

PIC NICS ON HAND.

East Avenue Baptist Church, Newport.

United Presbyterian Church, Newport.

North Street M. E. Sunday School, Newport.

Lake Avenue Baptist Church, Newport.

North Presbyterian Church, Newport.

St. Joseph's Church, Sea Breeze Grove.

Central Church, Sea Breeze Grove.

Asbury Church, Newport.

Eighth Ward Mission S. S.

A number of other Societies on hand. We have a neat, clean grove that can't be excelled in Western New York. Excursionists can have Steamers on the Bay at Low Rates.

Before completing arrangements don't fail to get my rates.

Yours Respectfully,

J. D. SCOTT,

No. 5 POWERS BLOCK, FIRST FLOOR,   *General Contracting Agent.*

BURNETT & WRIGHT, 38 EXCHANGE ST.

This handbill was created by Captain Scott to promote Sunday school "Pleasure Parties." The Newport House was a most desirable destination, as was the Grove for picnics at Sea Breeze. Tickets were sold from a booth at the Four Corners, in front of the Powers Block.

This rare photograph of the steamer *North King* shows it with a full head of steam and a great trail of smoke leaving its funnel. Steam powered the two massive side-wheels that had paddles to drive the vessel through the lake waters.

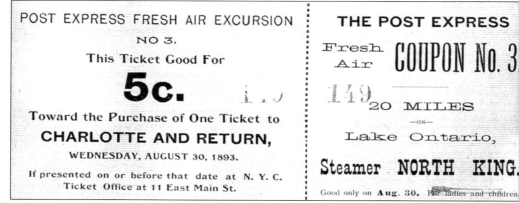

POST EXPRESS FRESH AIR EXCURSION

NO 3.

This Ticket Good For

5c.

Toward the Purchase of One Ticket to

CHARLOTTE AND RETURN,

WEDNESDAY, AUGUST 30, 1893.

If presented on or before that date at N. Y. C. Ticket Office at 11 East Main St.

THE POST EXPRESS

Fresh Air **COUPON No. 3**

149 20 MILES

—ON—

Lake Ontario,

Steamer **NORTH KING.**

Good only on **Aug. 30.** For ladies and children

On August 30, 1893, the steamer carried a large cargo of youngsters on a 20-mile "fresh air excursion" on Lake Ontario. The 5¢ voyage was sponsored by Rochester's newspaper, the *Post Express*.

There was sufficient ship traffic at the Charlotte harbor on the Genesee River to keep officers in the customhouse busy, especially during the summer vacation season. Much of the traffic came from Ontario Lake steamers transporting Rochesterians to resorts at Niagara Falls, the Thousand Islands, Kingston, Alexandria Bay, Toronto, and Montreal.

The good ship *Rochester*, which was new *c.* 1905, is seen leaving the port of Charlotte on a voyage that carried Victorian passengers to the Thousand Islands.

The *Ontario I*, seen here, and its sister ship, the *Ontario II*, were combination coal-car ferries and passenger ships. They plied the waters of Lake Ontario between Rochester and Cobourg, Ontario, with passenger service starting in 1909 and ending in 1950. The vessels were operated by the Ontario Car Ferry Company, a joint venture between the Canadian Grand Trunk Railroad and the Buffalo, Rochester & Pittsburgh Railroad. Pennsylvania coal was transported in 28 hopper cars, each weighing 68 tons. They were loaded aboard at the Genesee dock and shipped to the rail yard at Cobourg Harbor.

A photograph of the *Ontario I* bridge and pilot house reveals deck chairs occupied by a few of the 1,000 passengers that the vessel could accommodate. For a $1.25 special-excursion, round-trip ticket, travelers took memorable voyages across Lake Ontario. Aboard the *Ontario II*, voyagers enjoyed a promenade deck and perhaps the use of one of the 24 staterooms, a 32-seat dining room, the music room for dancing, or the large parlor. A ramp was built in 1927, allowing automobiles to be placed on flatcars, then taken aboard for transport to Cobourg, Ontario.

The *Ontario I* is seen pulling away from the mouth of the Genesee River on its way to Cobourg, Ontario. The great white vessel, with its buff and black-painted smokestacks, was the largest and most impressive ship of its day on Lake Ontario.

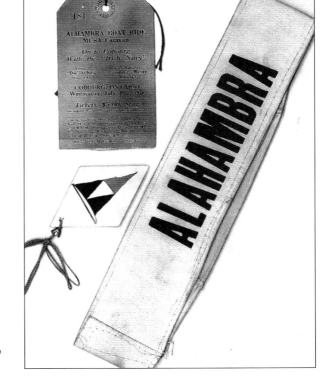

The members of the Alahambra Musa Caravan enjoyed a full day of entertainment on Wednesday, July 28, 1926. As the ticket for the *Ontario II* indicates, it was a stag party and each member was given a white sailor's hat imprinted with "Alahambra" on one side and "Rochester, N.Y." on the other. The ticket's schedule indicates that they had ample time to whoop it up in Colbourg.

A mule-hauled freight boat glides over the Genesee River aqueduct in this c. 1910 photograph. In a view looking west, the 11-story Wilder Building is seen in the top center and the old city hall tower rises on the skyline on the left. The canal bend was the tightest turn on the entire Erie Canal. The Erie Canal officially opened in 1825, with the last of the venerable animal-pulled boats plodding through downtown Rochester in 1918.

Horse-drawn wagons had to wait while canal boats passed under the Exchange Street lift bridge. The stairway on the left allowed pedestrians to cross without waiting. In 1904, Alling and Cory (now Expedx), on the left, occupied the building where the war memorial now stands.

This remarkable aerial photograph, a view looking north, is worth examining. It reveals the drained Erie Canal as it appeared in 1918, when its course took it through the center of Rochester. The former city hall and county courthouse are in the center, Exchange Street is on the right, Fitzhugh Street is in the center, and Plymouth Avenue is on the left. The entire canal bed, seen here, was covered over to form Broad Street. The deepened canal bed became a tunnel for the subway, exiting beyond the main library to the east. (Tom Kirn, New York Museum of Transportation collection, courtesy of the Rochester chapter NRHS.)

The packet boat C.S. *Tanner*, out of Port Byron, lies tied up at city hall. In a view looking east, the Exchange Street bridge can be seen in the distance. A jumble of barrels and planks lines the city hall dock on the left. The canal that passed city hall eventually became Broad Street.

In the foreground, the aqueduct crosses the Genesee River. The Court Street Bridge is on the left. The aqueduct was the longest on the Erie Canal. William S. Kimball's Peerless Tobacco Works building, occupied by the Cluett Peabody Shirt and Collar Company at the time this photograph was taken, dominates the scene in the right center.

In a view looking west past a moored freight boat is the old Erie Canal weigh lock, built in 1852 to replace an earlier one. The Commerce and Granite Buildings are seen in the center distance. Stone yards were located along the canal for shipping convenience.

Walter C. Cassebeer, a local architect and artist, sketched this fine detail of Rochester's weigh lock. Metal rods were attached to a huge scale with a cradle that freight boats floated over. The water was drained, then its tonnage weighed to determine its toll charge. The handsome Greek-Revival structure, with its dignified portico and Doric columns, was located on the east side of the canal opposite Capron Street.

A 200-foot towline is attached to a pair of mules that can be seen on the extreme left. The freight boat being pulled is just coming into sight were the canal bends. On the left, the Johnson and Seymour mill canal separates the canal from the Genesee River.

Hill's Basin on the Erie Canal is in the foreground. The weigh lock is west in the photograph. On the left is a lumberyard, with freight cars on the Erie Railroad just beyond. The photograph, c. 1900, was recorded from the Griffith Street bridge. (Courtesy of the Rochester chapter NRHS.)

The *Excelsior*, a steam-powered dredge, scoops out huge volumes of the Erie Canal's muddy sediment during the canal's enlargement. This *c.* 1920s scene is just south of Rochester.

This *c.* 1926 photograph shows the tugboat *Refuge* out of Rochester. Dozens of these tugs pushed freight barges on the canal. The *Refuge* served the barge canal terminal facility on the Genesee River just south of Court Street.

Pictured here is the barge canal terminal facility on the canal near Chili Avenue, adjoining the Buffalo, Rochester & Pittsburgh Railroad's yards at Lincoln Park. The electric hoist is lifting cargo from the motor ship *I.L.I. 103*, one of the largest vessels in the Chicago-New York lake and canal service.

This rare image is a ledger page from the Brockport Canal collector's office. Dated October 9, 1829, the old document discloses that N. Rowbuck, master of the *Seneca Chief* out of Albany, owed the collector $13.59. The cargo included three barrels of oysters. One hopes the oysters were fresh when they were delivered.

Two

HORSES AND
HORSE-DRAWN VEHICLES

Horses provided the major source of transportation during Rochester's early development. This illustration, originally drawn for the Paine Drug Company, depicts Rochester's first railway, powered, of course, by horses. Built by Elijah Johnson, the three-mile-long route connected flour mills on the upper Genesee River near the aqueduct, traveling on the east side of the river gorge, to Carthage, a bustling river hamlet located just north of the Genesee's lower falls. This point was as far upriver as lake schooners could navigate. The unique transportation line operated from 1833 to 1838.

A horse-drawn omnibus, or stagecoach, is seen arriving from a railway station. The passengers are staying at the Livingston Hotel on Exchange Street.

In the era prior to electric trolleys, West Main Street abounded with horse-drawn vehicles. Bobtail horse cars were the major means of transportation for riders between 1869 and 1892. (Courtesy of the New York Museum of Transportation.)

The city's horse-car line was started in 1862 by the Rochester City & Brighton Railroad Company. The first line was constructed from Elwanger and Barry's Nursery on Mount Hope Avenue, with old dobbin lumbering down to the driving park on Lake Avenue. The fare was 5¢, and the speed limit was seven miles per hour. In 1889, it became the Rochester Railway Company. The line had grown, employing 183 cars and 849 horses with routes covering many of the city's principle downtown and residential streets. (Chuck Whalen photograph courtesy of the Rochester chapter NRHS.)

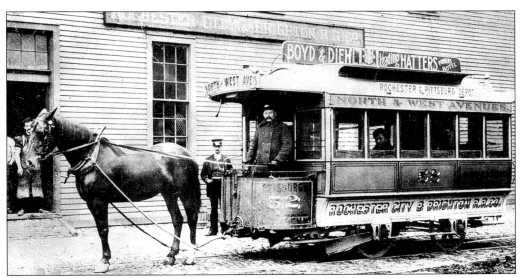

This faded image of horse car No. 52 on the Rochester City & Brighton Railroad line was taken in March 1867. A single horse pulled the tiny car that could accommodate about 15 passengers. Horse-car transportation provided a relatively smooth ride over iron rails when compared to jouncing over the city's Medina paving stones in a wagon.

This photograph, taken June 15, 1900, shows the elaborate, triumphal arch built at the intersection of East Main Street and East Avenue. It was a part of the city's gala welcome home for its returning Spanish-American war hero, Maj. Gen. Elwell S. Otis. Few cities have ever provided a more extensive reception than that given to General Otis, a Rochester native whose home was on Lyell Avenue.

Hundreds of Rochesterians lined Main Street to see General Otis and his handsome carriage drawn by a team of six matched horses. In the carriage facing the general is Mayor James G. Cutler and H.B. Hathaway, president of the chamber of commerce. Spanish-American War veterans and officers from the police department are marching as honor guards for the general. The parade was so lengthy it took most of the day to complete.

WORK HORSE PARADE
ROCHESTER INDUSTRIAL EXPOSITION
OCTOBER 15, 1909

Horses played such an extensive role in the transportation of the city's citizens and its goods that they were featured in a special parade held on October 15, 1909. It was a much-enjoyed segment of the city's annual industrial exposition.

Throngs of parade watchers are seen as the horse parade passes the white painted Bijou Dream Theater on the left, the city's first nickelodeon. It is not certain if the large vat atop the decorated wagon, drawn by eight horses each with a groom, represents beer or milk. The banner indicates that Rochesterians consumed 6,500 gallons of the liquid daily.

Throngs of visitors poured into Rochester to attend conventions in the early 1900s. Many hired Edward F. Higgins, "the Empire State's greatest livery," to employ their 20th-century "Tally Ho" for a ride around the Flower City. The Tally Ho seated 50 people, it was "the largest in the world," and it was drawn by eight beautiful horses. This early photograph records a visit to Highland Park.

At one time, Rochester's Four Corners, where Main Streets East and West crossed Exchange and State Streets, was considered to be one of the busiest traffic intersections in America. The rail pattern installed in 1893 accommodated trolley traffic with the first 12-way crossing, called the Grand Union. The traffic officer really has his hands full in this c. 1910 photograph.

Flower City . .
Gentlemen's Driving Assn.

SEASON
1899

MEMBERSHIP TICKET.

Mr. *Dr. J. Oliver Tait*

Chas. J. Chapin.
President.

James L. Hotchkiss.
Secretary.

Horse racing and driving a matched pair of attractive Arabian racers was as big a thrill to Victorians as driving racecars and sports cars is to racers today. In Rochester, the Flower City Gentlemen's Driving Association was a hot ticket in 1899. It was an elite group who took vast pride in owning and driving fine horses. The association's president was Charles T. Chapin.

Connor and Dariel were two of the finest thoroughbred horses in Rochester. Note how proudly they stood for this photograph in 1904. One can almost hear the jingling of harness bells, as Charles T. Chapin drove his sleigh over the city's icy streets.

HORSE SHOW AND RACES

CRITTENDEN PARK
-- (Old Fair Grounds.) --
now Crittenden Blvd--

Tuesday, Wednesday, Thursday and Friday

JUNE 23, 24, 25, 26

$5,600—IN PRIZES—$5,600

THE FASTEST TEAM IN THE WORLD OWNED BY ONE MAN

3-RACES DAILY-3

GRAND SHOW OF HORSES

Music by HEBING.

ADMISSION, 50 CENTS
Ladies Free. *1903* Carriages Free.

MILTON CLARK, Pres.   EDWARD L. FIEN, Treas.   THEO. H. COLEMAN, Secretary.

☞ South Ave. Cars Run Direct to Grounds

In April 1903, this poster drew sulky racing fans to Rochester's Crittenden Park, where ladies could attend for free. The prize money was considerable for the times. The race featured Charles T. Chapin and, as the poster indicates, "the finest team in the world owned by one man."

To arrive at Crittenden Park, many fans took the South Avenue trolley cars that ran directly to the park. The racetrack was a part of the former Monroe County Fairgrounds. Much of the area is now occupied by Strong Memorial Hospital. Fair buildings and stables are on the left in this photograph. The view looks west on Crittenden Boulevard from Mount Hope Avenue.

One did not need to go to a racetrack to witness a good horse race. Rochester's winter sleigh races were a frequent sight on East and Lake Avenues. The sleigh race in this photograph took place between two Corn Hill physicians.

Those seeking to buy a good sleigh to race on Rochester's snow-packed streets had no farther to look than the Caley and Nash Carriage and Sleigh Manufactory at the northwest corner of Winton Road and East Avenue. Superior sleighs were constructed in the former Brighton Village, at the intersection known as Caley's Corners. This photograph, dated 1892, displays an East Avenue that is unpaved.

Rochesterians who wanted coal delivered to their homes at the turn of the 20th century had it delivered in a wagon similar to those lined up in this photograph, taken of the Louis C. Langie Coal Company in 1904. Louis C. Langie, founder of the company in 1872, may be the gentlemen in the derby hat on the left of the wagon. The company's location appears to be at 502 North Street.

The venerable horse was employed to pull milk and bread wagons. The city used the steeds right into the 1940s. Horses pulled sidewalk snowplows and hauled refuse wagons, such as the one pictured coming up Falls Street from the incinerator. The Rochester Gas and Electric's station No. 3 (Beebee Station) is seen in the background.

Throughout the Victorian era, horses conveyed the populace by pulling many types of carriages, from the impressive wagon with the large kerosene lamp seen on the left to the stagecoach on the right. This photograph was taken in 1934 at Edgerton Park during the Rochester Centennial Exposition.

The lineup of vintage carriages shown here would be almost impossible to recreate today. However, in 1934, there were still many stored in local barns and carriage houses.

Higgin's Livery Stable prided itself on having one of the fanciest touring wagons available for hire. Called a Tally Ho, it was used to transport visitors and local folks on annual outings. In this c. 1890s photograph, 14 members of the Rochester Gas and Electric Company donned formal attire and squeezed aboard the wagon. That does not include the driver, groom, and the fellow standing in front of the wagon.

William J. Feisler is seen in front of his home at 19 Concord Street, between North and Merrimac Streets. Feisler was a farmer, shoemaker, and worked as a milkman when this photograph was taken c. 1911. Old dobbin, seen nuzzling his master, was Feisler's faithful milk-wagon horse.

This George B. Page and Son advertising card was designed to draw one's attention. The reverse of the advertisement lists more than 50 horse-related items available, including curry combs, buggy whips (Woodbury's of course), five-ring halters, harness polish, and Kendall's Spavin Cure.

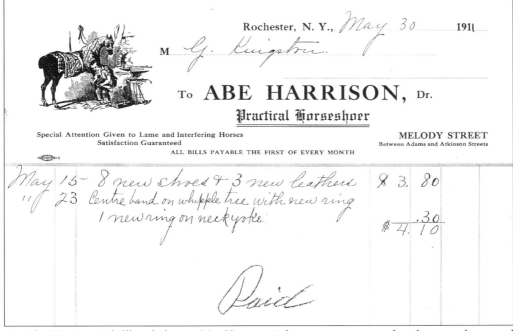

As Abe Harrison's billhead shows, Mr. Kingston's horse team received eight new shoes and assorted harness parts for $4.10 on May 30, 1911. Horseshoeing was done on Melody Street in old Corn Hill.

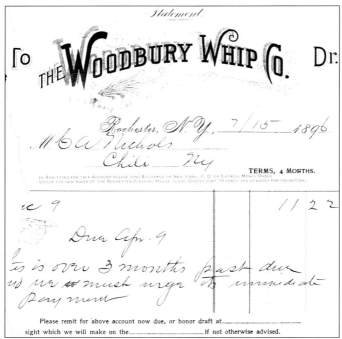

Just prior to the turn of the 20th century, the Woodbury Whip Company, at 111 Allen Street, led the nation in the production of fine buggy whips, producing 85,000 buggy, coach, riding, and team whips annually.

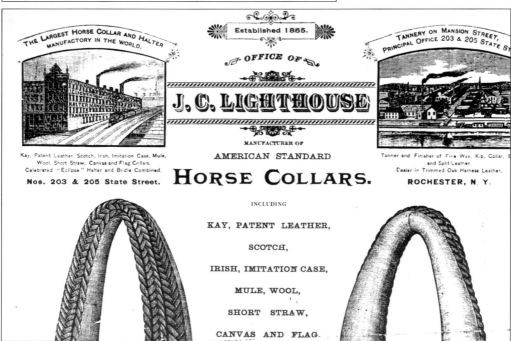

In 1865, John C. Lighthouse, the "Horse Collar King," built a tannery on Mansion Street on the Genesee River south of Corn Hill. It grew to become "the largest horse collar and halter manufactory in the world." Lighthouse amassed a fortune when his leather feed bags were redesigned, and thousands were purchased by the federal postal department to serve as mailbags on rural star routes.

This c. 1900 photograph is a view looking north down State Street from across the Four Corners intersection. Rochester's downtown teemed with horse, trolley, pedestrian, and bicycle traffic. The Elwood Building, with its tall gargoyle-spouting tower, is on the right.

Horse-drawn wagons were necessary to assure that William P. Buckley's Triangle Cafe and the Kelly Brother's lunchroom were well stocked with Bartholomay's Beer and Ale. The Liberty Pole now stands where this c. 1890 photograph was taken, at 302 East Main Street.

A dozen girls, dressed in boots and jodhpurs, have assembled with their steeds for a photograph taken on Saturday morning, June 10, 1933. The horse riders are all students, members of John Marshall High School's riding club. When was the last time a city high school sponsored an equestrian club?

The Rochester Fire Department's veterinary hospital was once located on Driving Park Avenue. Its task was to keep horses in fit condition, in an era when smoke-puffing steam-engine pumpers were drawn by horses to the fire scene. Seen here are, from left to right, Thomas Nolan, William Martin, Frank Doyle (in uniform), and Eugene Gilmore. The horses are, from left to right, George, King Tut, Poodle, Mugs, Bob, Jerry, Preny, and Sham.

Three
BICYCLES AND WHEELMEN'S CLUBS

The intersection of East Main Street and St. Paul Street is shown in this *c.* 1903 photograph. Members of a Rochester wheelmen's club cycle east on Main Street. A banner stretches across the street and advertises a steamer excursion from Charlotte to Canada for $1. The bicycle craze hit Rochester in the 1890s. By the 1900s, many wheelmen's clubs had been formed for both men and women. (Courtesy of the New York Museum of Transportation.)

Francis L. Hughes owned a four-story building on Exchange Street where he manufactured Crescent Bicycles. According to this advertisement, he produced 65,000 bicycles in 1896 and manufactured "700 each day in 1897." The price for a Crescent Bicycle, $50, was quite an outlay at the time.

The bicycle craze in Rochester was so strong in the 1890s that several local firms began production of the two-wheeled vehicles. At the time, little kids were seen wearing small pin-back buttons displaying a colorful humming bird. It was part of an advertising campaign for the Humming Bird Bicycle. The Bettys and Mabbett Company, the Humming Bird's manufacturer, promoted their 1896 model with this advertisement.

In this photograph, taken on a summer day *c.* 1900, a huge crowd gathers at the Rochester Driving Park's racetrack to witness a popular new sport: bicycle racing. The banner bedecked, three-story judge's stand was a predominant vantage point for watching the five-racer heat, as the contestants "scorched" around the track on their wheels. Some betting may have also been a part of the festivities.

One of the most unusual races ever held at the Rochester Driving Park was a match between Hattie E., a trotting mare, and Elsa Von Blumen, a lady bicyclist. Throngs of Rochesterians arrived, confident that a trotting horse could outrace a woman on a high-wheeler bicycle. Von Blumen won. (Sketch by Burt Miller.)

A *c.* 1910 bicycle race was organized for the boys in Rochester's Western Union telegraph service.

This *c.* 1905 photograph reveals six cheerful members of a local wheelmen's club. The lads are raising schooners of suds to cool off after their warm ride out to Manitou Beach Park.

Bicycle Kodaks.

$5.00, $8.00, $10.00, $25,00.

NOTHING SO FITS INTO THE PLEASURES OF BICYCLING AS PHOTOGRAPHY.

**Pocket Kodaks,
Cartridge Kodaks,
Bullets and
Bulls=Eyes**

are especially adapted to use awheel. They use our light-proof Film Cartridges and can therefore be

LOADED IN DAYLIGHT.

They are the lightest and most compact cameras made, and with our perfected bicycle carrying cases are entirely out of the way yet instantly available for use.

"Bicycle Kodaks" is the title of a little booklet that tells all about them. Free for the asking.

$2,853.00 In Prizes for
Kodak Pictures.
$1,475.00 in Gold.
*Send for "Prize Contest"
Circular.*

EASTMAN KODAK CO.

Rochester, N. Y.

Where but in the "Kodak City" would a company respond to the bicycle craze sweeping the area in the 1890s? With his Bicycle Kodak firmly attached to his wheel, a beau could ride with his sweetheart to the park or countryside for a picnic and record the romantic outing for a lifetime.

When the lads from the University of Rochester played baseball at the South Park ball grounds (Genesee Valley Park), mobs of supporters arrived by bicycle to root them on. In a view looking east, the Genesee River is in the background in this *c.* 1895 photograph.

The bicycle parked on West Main Street was a common sight *c.* 1910. A wave of enthusiastic bicyclists quickly adopted the newest transportation mode. After all, bicycles did not need oats, hay, or a stable. Flag-bedecked on the left is the Duffy-MacInerney Department Store. (Photograph by George H. Monroe.)

Four
TROLLEY AND AMUSEMENT PARK LINES

The era of horse cars ended by 1890. Larger trolleys were now rolling down Rochester's main streets and electricity replaced old dobbin. The immaculately uniformed motorman and conductor were responsible for service on trolley No. 466. Note the neat "cow-catcher" attached to the front of the trolley.

Open-sided trolley cars, built for fair-weather service, once took riders to amusement parks, ball games, and events at the Rochester Driving Park. This c. 1908 photograph shows motormen and conductors returning to the carbarn on State Street owned by the New York Railways Company.

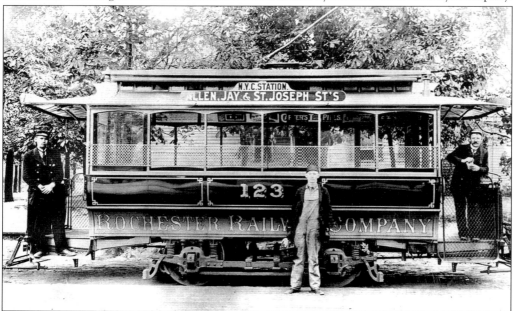

This early model trolley had but one wheel set. It was reported that these units were built by placing new trucks under the former horse cars. The trolley operated along Allen, Jay, and St. Joseph (Joseph Avenue) Streets and picked up passengers at the New York Central depot.

ROCHESTER RAILWAY CO.
TRANSFER TICKET.
ISSUED ON LINE PUNCHED. + 40 + TRADE-MARK.
Good for this current trip from Line punched, over any other Line, if used on first car within 10 MINUTES of the time punched; subject to Rules of Company.
(OVER.)

№ 75249   Issued by Conductor No. **454**

Jan.	Feb.	March	April	May	June	July	Aug.	Sept.	Oct.	Γ	.	Dec.
1	2	3	4	5	6	7	8	9	10	11	12	13 14 15
16	17	18	19	20		22	23	24	25	26	27	28 29 30 31

Hudson	& Exc.	South	& Lake	X	X	Univer.	& Lyell	South	Clinton
Monroe	&	North	& West	East &	West	N. St. P.	& Sophia	Gen'se	Street
Clinton	& Jeff.	Ridge	Road	Park	Ave.	Allen &	St. Jos.	*	*

	1	2	3	4	5
1	1	2	3	4	5
2	1	2	3	4	5
3	1	2	3	4	5
4	1	2	3	4	5
5	1	2	3	4	5
6	1	2	3	4	5
7	1	2	3	4	5
8	1	2	3	4	5
9	1	2	3	4	5
10	1	2	3	4	5
11	1	2	3	4	5
12	1	2	3	4	5

The trolley-car transfer was originated in Rochester in August 1892. Its creator, John Harry Stedman, devised a small paper transfer showing seven rider profiles, as well as their destination, sex, month, age (plus or minus 40), and the date of travel. The transfer was to enable conductors to better spot riders exceeding their fare limits. Riders had 10 minutes to transfer to a car heading on a different route.

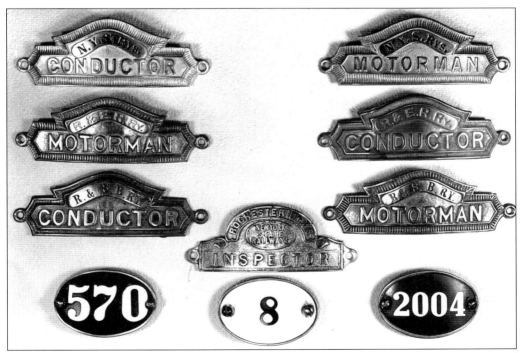

This image shows trolley-car cap badges from the New York Railways, Rochester & Eastern Rapid Railway, and Rochester & Sodus Bay Railroad. Also seen are an inspector's badge for the New York Railway, a No. 570 badge (for a Rochester Railways conductor), a No. 8 badge (a novice), and a No. 2004 badge (which belonged to supervisor J. Perry). (William Gordon Collection.)

As can be noted, the Rochester & Suburban Railway Company charged fares for crossing Irondequoit Bay. The ferry receipt lists the types of vehicles, animal, or human passengers making the crossing.

A Rochester & Sodus Bay Railroad trolley can be seen heading east, approaching the Float Bridge over Irondequoit Bay. Known as Empire Boulevard today, the passage across the bay outlet was a narrow float bridge. The trolley service, known as the Royal Blue Line, lasted from 1889 to 1929.

As their banners indicate, these nurses were the graduating classes of 1908 and 1909, all employed at the Rochester Homeopathic Hospital. The ladies were off on a picnic at one of Rochester's five trolley amusement parks.

The ingenious Capt. George W. Ruggles of Charlotte stands next to his invention: a rotary snowplow. Designed in 1893, it had electric-powered fan blades to fight Rochester's winter snow drifts. Orders came from trolley companies throughout the northeast and Canada seeking delivery of his novel track cleaner. Joshua Vascell is aboard trolley car No. 20.

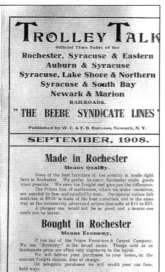

Two pamphlets were distributed by Rochester's trolley lines. *Trolley Topics* contained the "official timetables and guide for the Rochester Railway Co. and interurban lines." It carried advertisements, included jokes, and boasted its amusement trolley parks. *Trolley Talk* was a brochure distributed to its passenger by "the Beebe Syndicate Lines." This company ran interurban trolleys from Rochester to Auburn, Syracuse, Newark, Marion, and points east. It too contained timetables, advertisements, and jokes.

Two pages from a *Trolley Topics* brochure represent some of the content. It allowed trolley passengers to learn about the yacht-race schedule for Irondequoit Bay, as well as the Rochester baseball team's home and away schedule for 1907. The joke is pretty corny. Note the price of a demijohn of rye.

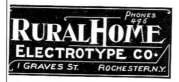

Looking very natty with his blue suit, gold buttons, and change maker on his belt, the conductor worked for the New York Railways Company. It was a respected occupation in its day.

It was May 9, 1935, when this trolley car swung around the loop in Genesee Valley Park. Car No. 1003 was built by the G.C. Kuhlman Company in 1913 for the New York Railways Company. (Courtesy of the New York Museum of Transportation.)

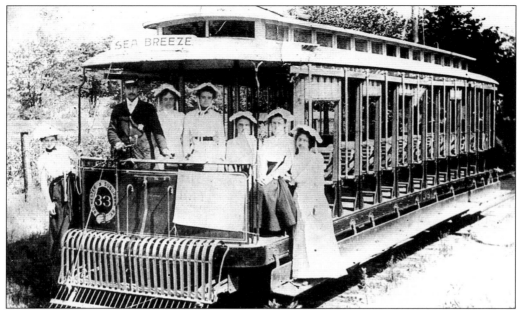

Bound for the Mignonette Cottage at Sea Breeze, the six Blue Bonnet Girls were photographed *c.* 1900 with motorman Fred A. Banham, who worked for the Rochester & Suburban Railway. As members of the Blue Bonnet Club, each girl wore a long white dress and a fancy blue bonnet. The members, from left to right, are Sophie Fox, Irene Dodson, Louise Foos, Emily Engler, Belle Miller, and Effie Dukelow.

In winter, a small stove served to take the biting chill off those passengers near enough to the heat source. At several locations along the trolley routes were roadside depots where men provided scuttles of coal for the trolley stoves. This was not the most enviable occupation on the trolley line, but one acquired a lot of fresh air.

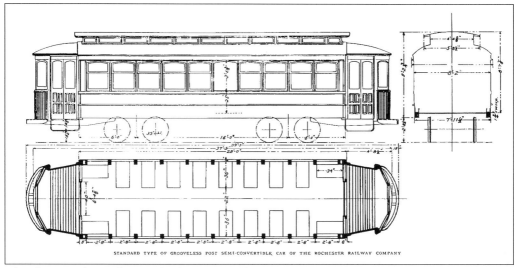

STANDARD TYPE OF GROOVELESS POST SEMI-CONVERTIBLE CAR OF THE ROCHESTER RAILWAY COMPANY

This diagram shows the standard type of Brill Groveless Post Semi-Convertible car built by the G.C. Kuhlman Car Company for the Rochester Railway Company. Chartered on July 9, 1887, it became one of America's pioneer lines. Forty five of the cars were delivered and forty more were under construction. (*Brill's Magazine*, Volume 1, No. 1; January 15, 1907.)

This 1926 G.C. Kuhlman Company trolley car is just turning the loop at Hudson Avenue. This photograph was taken on a warm day, August 11, 1934, by Wallace Bradley. (Courtesy of the New York Museum of Transportation.)

In 1910, when this popular song told the world that Rochester was "a grand old city," a photograph of Main Street was featured on the sheet-music cover illustrating the city's vitality abounding with trolley and pedestrian traffic. Trolleys are seen passing the Bijou Dream Theater, Mc Farlin's Clothing Store, and the Burke, Fitzsimmons, and Hone buildings on the left. The tall building on the left is the Granite Building on the northeast corner of East Main and St. Paul Streets. The chorus is, "Rochester Made that means Quality with me You'll all agree Rochester! Take me there! It's the city where I want to be."

54

This vivid reminder of yesterday reveals North Street as it appeared *c.* 1914. On the left is Sibley's Terminal Building (the Tower Building). One of its spaces has been leased to the Guilford Drug Company. On the right is the steeple of the Second Baptist Church on Franklin Street. On the lower right is the triangle block, today's location of the Liberty Pole. Both automobiles and trolleys share the road with a diminishing number of horse-drawn wagons. (Courtesy of the New York Museum of Transportation.)

The photograph looks south where South Clinton Avenue meets East Main Street. On the left is the East Side Savings Bank. Just beyond the bank is the Seneca Hotel. Trolley traffic is competing with the increase of automobile ownership. On the lower right, an impatient motorist is trying to pass a trolley. (Courtesy of the Rochester chapter NRHS.)

Here is where trolley No. 558 and a shiny new 1927 Buick automobile "traded paint," and a little more. It appears as though the automobile attempted to pass the trolley on its right and ran out of room. The advertisement on the trolley reads, "Victoria Theater, Lon Chaney in *Tell It To The Marines.*" (Courtesy of Jack Kemp.)

Remember when the trolleys rumbled down Dewey Avenue? If not, think about that romantic mode of transportation. One could always tell when a trolley car was approaching from its rolling thunder and the clang, clang of its bell. Trolley car No. 2002 is seen turning the corner onto Driving Park Avenue, where Morris Wichman ran the cut-rate drug store.

Rochester continually improves the condition of its streets. It is hard to recognize the tree-lined East Main Street in this *c.* 1910 photograph. Laying paving bricks between the trolley tracks was a highly labor-intensive occupation.

To support the heavy traffic on Exchange Street, the city installed large blocks of red Medina sandstone as pavers. Post's Drug Store is on the left. The facade of the Powers Building can be seen beyond it. This *c.* 1910 photograph is a view looking north toward State Street.

This postcard, dated 1913, records the busy traffic at State and West Main Streets. Three trolleys can be counted sharing the intersection with later forms of transportation modes. On the left are both an early motor bike and a vintage automobile. Pedestrians crossed at their own risk. This view looks north down State Street.

A trolley makes its way up East Main Street and passes the Granite Building on the right. The World War I-era postcard scene, dated May 14, 1918, was taken from Stone Street looking west. Pvt. Norman S. Burkhardt, United States Army Aerial Photography, Kodak Park, Dorm 14, writes to Miss Helen, "Have been here now for about 2 months studying aerial photography. Would be glad to hear from you."

The Rochester Trust and Safe Deposit Bank once had an impressive building on the southwest corner of Exchange and East Main Streets. The photograph, dated 1909, was taken when fewer than 200 "road machines" in Rochester vied for road space with trolley and horse traffic. A tiny, open-seated electric automobile is just entering Exchange Street.

Neatly lined up for inspection are three Rochester streetcars. A numbering system helps identify when the trolleys entered service: 1906: No. 600–639; 1912: No. 1000–1024; 1914: No. 850–869; and 1916: No. 1200–1249.

From November 1923 through March 1932, the Rochester Railway Co-ordinated Bus Lines put 12 unique "trackless trolleys" into service. The trolley chassis was made in Cortland by the Brockway Truck Company, the body made by Kuhlman of Cleveland, Ohio. A unique overhead crossing device was developed here, allowing trackless trolley lines to cross regular trolley lines. This "trolley-bus" operated on a cross-town route across Driving Park Bridge. Fare was 8¢. Note the hard-riding, solid rubber tires.

At 60 miles per hour, an interurban car of the Rochester & Eastern Rapid Railway is challenging a New York Central & Hudson River Railroad train on parallel tracks between Rochester and Canandaigua.

We are so used to buses pulling right up to the curb, we may have forgotten that street-centered trolley tracks caused passengers to line up on "islands" in the middle of the street. In a common 1930s scene along East Main Street, long queues await the trolley in front of Woolworth's. The store was once located in the Granite Building at the northeast corner of East Main and St. Paul Streets. (Courtesy of the New York Museum of Transportation.)

The clothing, white shoes, and hats seen in this trolley queue hearken back to the 1930s, when passengers awaited to board trolleys that stopped near the front of Sibley's Department Store.

These colorful weekly passes, issued by the New York Railways Company and later by the Rochester Transit Corporation, were first used by trolley and later by bus commuters. Available from 1935 through the late 1950s, they advertised coming events, gave historical and safety information, and promoted patriotism during World War II. Today, these elusive bits of yesterday have become treasured collector's items for transportation and local history buffs.

A lone trolley trundles east on the Court Street Bridge crossing the Genesee River in this 1909 photograph. A horse and buggy follows behind. It is a nostalgic scene, with trolleys gone now for more than six decades and horse transportation far longer. Only a few are left who remember the heyday of electric trolleys rumbling down our streets, snapping and spitting sparks as their trolley wheels arced over trolley-wire intersections. It was all a part of Rochester's golden yesterdays.

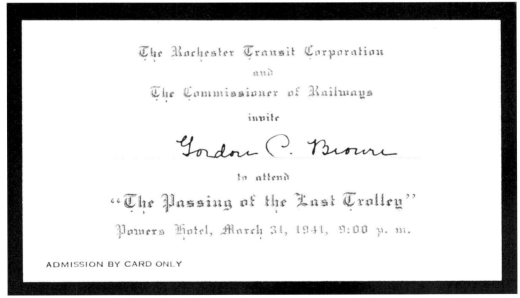

The Rochester Transit Corporation

and

The Commissioner of Railways

invite

Gordon C. Brown

to attend

"The Passing of the Last Trolley"

Powers Hotel, March 31, 1941, 9:00 p. m.

ADMISSION BY CARD ONLY

As a final salute to Rochester's trolley era, this note was sent to leading members of the city. It marked "the passing of the last trolley." The black-edged invitation is a memento of the memorial service given at the Powers Hotel to say goodbye to the last trolley run on March 31, 1941, at 9:00 p.m. Gordon C. Brown was the owner of the WSAY radio station.

What ever happened to all those remarkable trolleys? A trolley can be identified at the left in this late 1940s photograph. The trolley has been transformed into Ethel's Diner. This view looks southeast with the Kodak Office Tower in the skyline.

Michelson's fender-dented Ford is parked in front of another city trolley that metamorphosed into a diner. In 1930, the trolley-diner was operated by Julius J. MacPherson at 178 South Fitzhugh Street.

Five

TRAINS AND RAIL STATIONS

Serving the Tonawanda Railroad, this quaint, wood-burning engine wheezed along the tracks, emitting clouds of smoke and sparks, at a speedy 10 miles per hour. Its maiden run was on April 4, 1837, when the train pulled out of the Tonawanda depot on Buffalo Street under the charge of conductor L.B. Van Dyke. It reached Churchville just 40 minutes later. The 15-foot, stagecoach-like cars each held 24 passengers and were built in the Rochester shops of the railway company by men who had never seen a railroad coach.

This sketch of Rochester's first locomotive was drawn by local architect and rail fan John Wenrich. Ironically, the little engine, a future competitor for canal freight and passengers, arrived in Rochester on an Erie Canal boat.

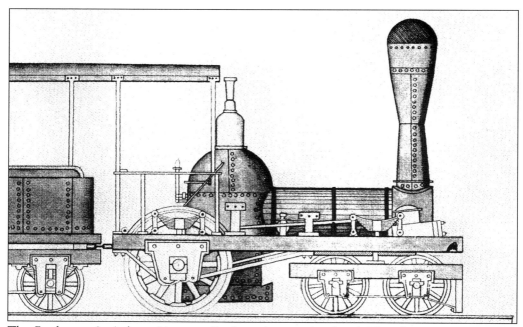

The Rochester & Auburn Line was Rochester's second railroad. This drawing represents its locomotive the *Young Lion*. It came to Rochester by way of the Erie Canal in 1840. Asa Goodale was the engineer, and Joseph Hoffman was the fireman. The coaches were called "elegant equipages." In 1840, the engines *Ontario* and *Columbus* also arrived by canal. The original drawing was presented to the Rochester Historical Society by the New York Central Railroad.

This odd-appearing engine had its original profile transformed into a trolley shape, supposedly in an effort not to alarm horses. The Baldwin 0-4-2 engine, built in 1884, hauled two cars on the old Rochester & Lake Ontario Railroad in 1890 from Bay Street down Portland Avenue to Ridge Road to Sea Breeze.

A party of bewhiskered railroad dignitaries is about to leave on an inspection tour of New York Central & Hudson River Railroad tracks in the Rochester area. Engine No. 513, a rare 4-2-4, progressed at a speed slow enough to allow the gentlemen seated in front of the engineer to obtain the best view of the railway right-of-way. (Courtesy of the Rochester chapter NRHS.)

The Piano World is located at Despatch are the largest in America.

N.Y.C.

Foster–Armstrong Piano Factory, A leading Industry. Despatch, N. Y.

I liked your cards very much

One of the major trackside industries attracted to East Rochester was the Foster-Armstrong Piano Factory, later the Aeolian American Corporation, seen in this rare postcard view dated July 1906. The four tracks of the New York Central's main line are in the foreground. According to the postcard sender, "the piano works . . . located in Despatch are the largest in America."

It was a great day on May 30, 1897, for Despatch (East Rochester), when scores of men turned out to witness the laying of the cornerstone for the new Merchants Despatch Transportation Company's car shops. The community, becoming Rochester's first industrial suburb, attracted a number of important industries. Derby hats were the order of the day.

Workmen at the East Rochester car shops labored long for their few dollars. The trio in this 1920 photograph appears in front of the main carbarn. A set of railroad-car wheels can be seen behind them.

By 1899, the Merchants Despatch Transportation Company, employing 700 workers, was manufacturing strings of white-painted refrigerator cars. In this faded 1900 photograph, the lettering indicates that the recently built cars were sold to the Lehigh Valley and the Dairy Line. Everyone in Victorian times usually wore a hat when at work. The men appear happy to be photographed.

Calling itself "the Convention City" in 1910, the Rochester Chamber of Commerce made every effort to attract conventioneers to the city, especially by rail, then the most available form of transportation. The neatly clad gentlemen in the photograph are poised to greet convention-bound passengers disembarking from an Erie Railroad coach.

ROCHESTER, N.Y.

THE CONVENTION CITY

The cover of this 1910 Rochester Chamber of Commerce brochure was designed to induce tourists and conventioneers to the city by railroad. The 16-page booklet presented a downtown map, photographs of available accommodations, and points of pride and interest.

This perspective more clearly shows the three arches of the vintage train shed. Earlier, the Auburn & Rochester Railroad used the site for its depot. On February 18, 1861, at this site, Abraham Lincoln addressed the Rochester public from the observation platform of his official train while on its journey to Washington for Lincoln's inauguration. Lincoln's speech was brief, but was heard by one of the largest crowds on the president's entire trip to the Capitol.

The huge, half-round-shaped train shed was the first New York Central Station on Mill Street, from 1854 through 1883. In this c. 1870s view looking east is the station, west of the Genesee River between Mill and State Streets. On the left, the white building is the New York Central's Rochester offices. Engine No. 166 is steaming up as it departs the train shed. The Savoy Hotel's wrought-iron balcony can be seen on the right. The sign advertises raw oysters for 25¢ and milk stew for 35¢.

A second station was built by the New York Central & Hudson River Railroad in 1882 at a cost of $925,000. Huge iron arches now supported the newest train shed. The tracks pass over St. Paul Street. In 1882, Rochester elevated its railroad tracks to eliminate grade crossings. It was only the second such track-elevation program outside of New York City in the entire nation.

The 1910 photograph captures the large red-brick structure that greeted New York Central passengers when they arrived in Rochester. Built in 1883, the depot was moved to the east side of the Genesee River between St. Paul Street and North Clinton Avenue along Central Avenue.

This turn-of-the-20th-century photograph shows the depot as it appeared in 1907. The depot was the entry point for thousands of travelers and immigrants seeking new lives in Rochester's industries and commercial establishments.

A site for a third New York Central Station was being sought by the late 1890s. The old station was in need of repair and enlargement. This photograph, taken from the railroad tower at the northeast corner of Joseph Avenue, appeared in the *Rochester Herald* in September 1910. It shows the area selected for a new depot. The old train sheds can be seen on the right. Joseph Avenue is on the left. The Schaefer Block is the large building in the center of the picture.

Claude Bragdon, Rochester's leading architect, was commissioned to design the third New York Central depot. His sketch shows the three large windows placed in the facade he conceived to remind travelers of the great driving wheels of a locomotive. In a view looking directly north from Central Avenue, the station exhibited an impressive, finely balanced exterior.

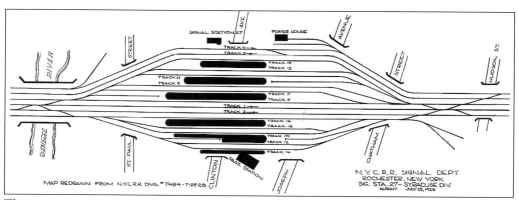

The great concentration of rails provided 16 tracks with platforms sporting graceful butterfly canopies that kept smoke, rain, and soot from passengers. The yard averaged 30 trains a day. (Diagram redrawn by Paul Jordan.)

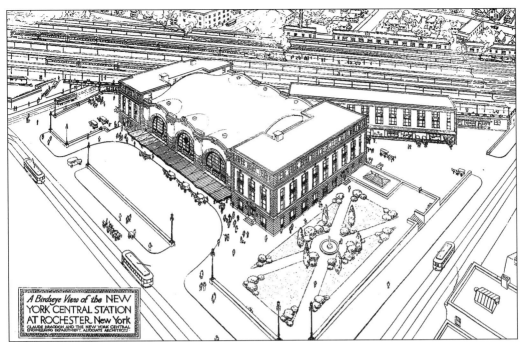

A Birdseye View of the NEW YORK CENTRAL STATION AT ROCHESTER. New York
CLAUDE BRAGDON AND THE NEW YORK CENTRAL
ENGINEERING DEPARTMENT, ASSOCIATE ARCHITECTS

As can be seen in this December 1913 pen-and-ink sketch by Claude Bragdon, the new station was an architectural treasure that any city would have been proud to claim.

This 1920s photograph was taken from the northeast corner of North Clinton and Central Avenues. Presidents Woodrow Wilson, Warren G. Harding, Calvin Coolidge, Franklin D. Roosevelt, Harry Truman, and Dwight D. Eisenhower were among those who used the station. Many spoke to huge crowds from a dais erected at the intersection.

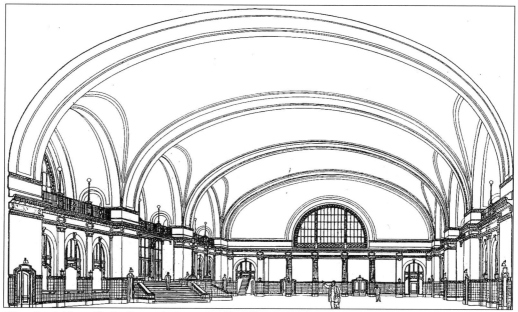

The third New York Central Station officially opened on January 19, 1914. On that date, 25,000 visitors arrived to view the new structure. Most were amazed by the spacious interior and impressed by the waiting room's 60-foot-high vaulted ceiling.

Long wooden benches lined the $2 million station's vast waiting room. Its wainscoting, nine feet high, was done in blue, green, and gold ceramic tiles. During World War II, hundreds of service men and women traveled by way of this station.

The depot's main entrance had steps leading down to the concourse floor. A barber shop, shoe-shine stand, and restaurant offered their services to Rochester's travelers.

In 1921, this photograph captured the passenger train yards of Rochester's New York Central Station. In a view looking east, in the right background is the station itself. On the left, the complex of canopies covered some of the 16 tracks that served the busy station. Rochester lost forever the noble structure when it was demolished in 1966. Most of the area became a parking lot. (Courtesy of the Rochester chapter NRHS.)

WEEK-END TOURS
TO
NEW YORK

NOVEMBER 4 - 11 - 18

Views of New York City

$15⁰⁰ ROUND TRIP from **BUFFALO**

$12⁵⁰ ROUND TRIP from **ROCHESTER**

$10⁰⁰ ROUND TRIP from **SYRACUSE**

Children Under 12 Half Fare; Under 5, Free

SPEND AN EXCITING WEEK-END IN THE WORLD'S GREATEST CITY
SCHEDULE

This travel poster, printed for the New York Central Railroad, encouraged western New Yorkers to take the train to New York City during Thanksgiving weekend in 1966. How modest the rail prices seem.

This Italianate house and its covered walkways once served as the Western New York & Pennsylvania Railroad station. That railroad had secured a lease from the earlier Genesee Valley Railroad. Its depot was located on West Main Street.

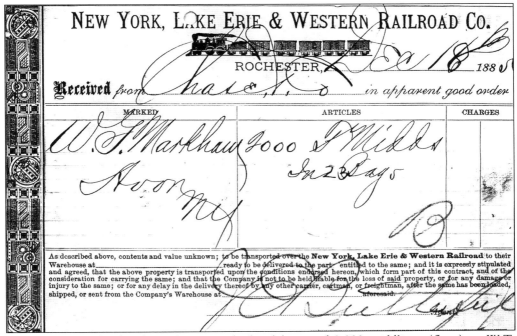

This bill of goods, dated 1885, was made for delivery of 2,000 middlings (flour) to W.T. Markham by way of the New York, Lake Erie & Western Railroad Company. That railroad, starting in 1878, was eventually absorbed by the Erie Railroad c. 1895.

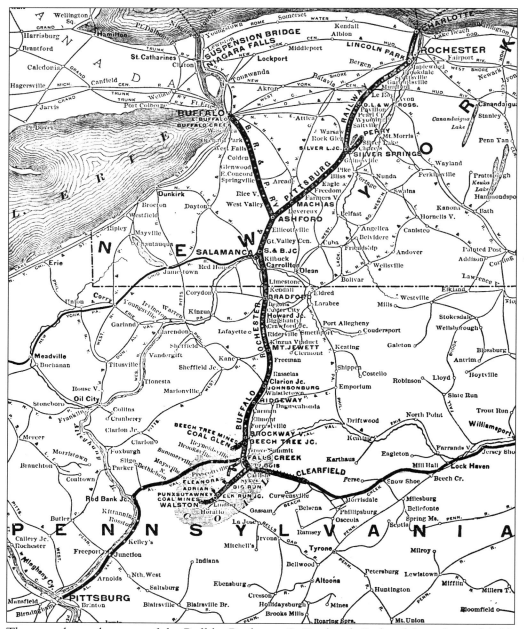

The map shows the route of the Buffalo, Rochester & Pittsburgh Railroad from the coal fields of Pennsylvania to Rochester's port at Charlotte, where coal was ferried to Cobourg, Ontario. The first load of coal went to Canada on November 11, 1907.

This banner-bedecked building at 155 West Main and Washington Streets held the general offices of the Buffalo, Rochester & Pittsburgh Railroad. The solid brick, five-story building continues to survive today.

This building at 320 West Main Street is familiar to all those who dine at Nick Tahoe's eating establishment. Originally the Rochester & State Line's depot, the building was greatly enlarged between 1881 and 1910 to accommodate the new owners. This may account for the structural differences in the end sections of the former depot. In 1931, the Baltimore & Ohio Railroad acquired control of the Buffalo, Rochester & Pittsburgh Railroad.

These crew members of the Buffalo, Rochester & Pittsburgh Railroad pose for this picture *c.* 1920. The location was the rail line's staging and maintenance yards at Lincoln Park on West Avenue.

Even employed in an occupation as demanding as railway workers had, there was still time for some of the crew, maintenance, and clerical employees to form a company baseball team. The uniforms look sharp, embroidered with the railway's initials. Most of the games were played against rival railroad teams at the ball grounds at Windsor Beach or the Newport House.

In the 1930s, the largest individual shipment of shoes ever sent out of Rochester consisted of 9,500 pairs of shoes valued at $75,000. They were shipped from the E.P. Reed Shoe Company for delivery on the Rochester, Buffalo & Pittsburgh Railroad to C.H. Baker Stores in San Francisco and Los Angeles, California.

One of the changes brought about when the Baltimore & Ohio succeeded the Rochester, Buffalo & Pittsburgh Railroad was the introduction of the gas-electric locomotive. This combination unit is departing the Baltimore & Ohio station heading for Salamanca c. 1940. Nick Tahoe's is seen in the background. (Courtesy of the Rochester chapter NRHS.)

This remarkable structure was a wooden trestle built in 1896 by the Buffalo, Rochester & Pittsburgh Railroad at Yates Dock. It was used to transfer coal from hopper cars to awaiting lake boats on the Genesee River. By 1909, improved facilities allowed 4,000 tons of coal a day to be loaded aboard using a 1,000-foot-long automatic coal chute. Empty hopper cars returned by the gravity track passed under the trestle. (Wallace Bradley photograph *c.* 1930, courtesy of the Rochester chapter NRHS.)

On a frosty morning *c.* 1945, a locomotive backs a string of coal-filled hopper cars onto the lower deck of the ferry boat *Ontario II*. The Baltimore & Ohio Railroad shipped coal to Cobourg, Ontario. (Wallace Bradley photograph, courtesy of the Rochester chapter NRHS.)

DELIGHTFUL LOW RATE

EXCURSION

— TO —

NIAGARA FALLS

Under the Auspices of the Alumni Association of the
SCOTTSVILLE PUBLIC SCHOOL,

WEDNESDAY, AUGUST 23, 1893

VIA THE

BUFFALO, ROCHESTER & PITTSBURGH R'Y

Fill your Lunch Baskets and Invite your friends to join
you in a day's outing at the Great Cataract.

SPECIAL TRAIN OF THROUGH COACHES

WILL RUN AS PER FOLLOWING SCHEDULE :

Stations.	Time.	Fare	Stations	Time	Fare
Rochester, -	8.15 A. M.	$1.50	Garbuttsville,	8.45 A. M.	$1.15
Scottsville,	8.40 "	1.25	Mumford, -	8.52 "	1.00

Arrive at Niagara Falls at 11 A. M. Returning, leave the Falls
from New York Central Station at 5.45 P. M.

Children between the Ages of 5 and 12 Years Half Fare

In 1893, iron rails and steam trains offered an escape to distant locations rarely reached by horse and buggy. This poster announces a "day's outing at the Great Cataract." To those happy citizens of Scottsville, the rail excursion and picnic was a benchmark in their lives, fondly recalled as the years passed by.

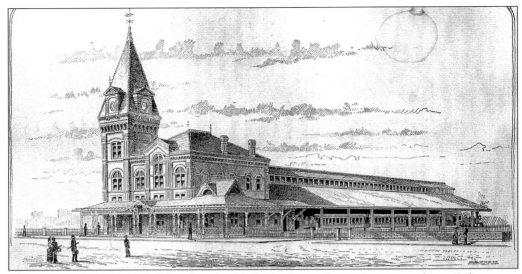

This vintage sketch is of the Erie depot c. 1888. Few knew the station as seen here. A four-story building blocked an eastern view of the extensive train sheds. The original Erie Railroad, begun in 1840, was wide gauge (six feet between the rails). It was built to deliver anthracite coal to Buffalo for shipment on the Great Lakes. In 1868, the Erie Railroad built its first freight house on Exchange Street.

Built in 1886, the Erie depot was located on Court Street on the Genesee's west bank. The Buffalo, New York & Erie Railroad leased the tracks from the former Rochester & Genesee Valley Railroad on October 1, 1858. Its four-story clock steeple became a local landmark.

Wagons travel west over the Court Street Bridge in this 1913 photograph. On the left is the towering Erie Railroad station. Beyond is the National Casket Company's factory. William S. Kimball's Peerless Tobacco Works is on the right. In the distance, a Rochester & Eastern interurban trolley is just entering Court Street.

In later years, c. the 1930s, the Erie Railroad station also served as the Rochester terminal for the Greyhound Bus Company. The station served as a convenient "intermodel" connection for train and bus passengers. Notice the price of a ticket to New York City.

It was a sad day for many rail fans when the grand old Erie Railroad station was razed. Passenger service had been discontinued for six years by the summer of 1947, when this photograph was taken. Today, the site serves as a parking lot for fans attending community war-memorial events. A small corner of the library can be seen across the river on the right. (Courtesy of the Rochester chapter NRHS.)

What a majestic sight this powerful steam engine must have been to both kids and grownups. Built by Rogers in 1905, the Erie K-1 Pacific was photographed by Wallace Bradley at the Erie station in January 1935. How many Rochesterians enjoyed riding behind the powerful No. 2521? (Courtesy of the Rochester chapter NRHS.)

Someone saved these small relics of the bygone days of the Erie Railroad. The reverse side of the New York to Rochester, Erie Railroad ticket is dated April 21, 1871. In 1901, the Erie Railroad operated a major maintenance facility in Avon, New York.

This little engine, once operated by the Gleason Works on University Avenue, was very unusual. It ran when its tank was filled with hot steam at the Gleason Works boiler house. Sometimes referred to as a "fireless cooker" or "hot water bottle," the engine was usually good for a day's yard switching. Further, it needed no coal or oil, produced no ashes, and was easy to operate.

Built in 1905 on the southwest corner of Court Street and South Avenue, the Lehigh Valley passenger station served Rochesterians for decades. The early motorist in this photograph is having trouble with his automobile. Perhaps he should have taken the train.

As this 1917 photograph shows, the Lehigh Valley station is cantilevered over the Genesee River. Little land was available to enter the city from the south. Today, a popular restaurant occupies the vintage station. The YMCA, which served as the railroad men's hotel, is in the background on the right. The old Osborn House Hotel on South Avenue is seen in the center skyline.

This *c.* 1930s photograph focuses on the Lehigh Valley's "doodlebug" No. 17. Built by the Osgood Bradley Company in 1929, it was designed for both freight and passenger service. This gas-electric unit brought many students to Rochester high schools from outlying villages and farms between the city and points south. The doodlebug operated until September 1950. The Lehigh's downtown approach was built over the old Johnson and Seymour mill race. (Tom Kirn collection, courtesy of the New York Museum of Transportation.)

An amateur photographer snapped this photograph of the Empire State Express coaches, as the New York Central train boarded passengers in Rochester on April 30, 1942. Today, six of these coaches have been restored for fall foliage excursions by the Rochester chapter of the National Railway Historical Society. (Photograph by Ernest Brians.)

The Rome, Watertown & Ogdensburg Railroad built this bridge across the Genesee River in the 1880s. It was the railroad's route into Rochester, with a terminal on North St. Paul Street in 1886. Note the sturdy stone column supporting the center of the bridge.

More than a century later, the bridge continued to serve rail traffic. A Conrail train WBRO-16 is seen crossing the venerable bridge in July 1985. Coal-filled hopper cars were delivered to the Beebee Station of the Rochester Gas and Electric Company on State Street. (Photograph by Ron Amberger, courtesy of the Rochester chapter NRHS.)

Six

THE ROCHESTER RAPID TRANSIT & INDUSTRIAL RAILWAY

In 1920, city engineer Edward A. Fisher was given the green light to plan an interurban and industrial railway, much of it located in the bed of the old Erie Canal. On July 24, 1925, city officials gathered to observe the progress being made on the Rochester Rapid Transit & Industrial Railway. Seen on the hand car, from left to right, are a subway worker; Edward A. Fisher, city engineer; John O'Connor, chief project engineer; and Clarence Van Zandt, Republican mayor of Rochester.

This candid photograph, taken from South Avenue *c.* 1923, reveals that work was well underway in the canal aqueduct bed. Workmen removed portions of the original walls to accommodate a four-rail subway route across the Genesee River.

Four subway rails emerge from the bed of the former Erie Canal aqueduct crossing the Genesee River. This striking photograph was taken after the completion of the project in September 1927. Today, the public library straddles the lower right of the photograph. One could feel the vibration as trolleys rumbled under the structure on tracks still in place beneath the library.

An inspection tour was arranged for the Rochester Engineering Society on October 17, 1926. The sightseers crammed aboard three flatcars and a caboose owned by I.M. Ludington and Son, who did much of the excavating and other work on the subway. This photograph was taken between Lyell Avenue and Felix Street. (Courtesy of the Rochester chapter NRHS.)

This photograph depicts three major forms of transportation: canal, rail, and subway. The subway tracks are seen on the lower right as they pass east of a ramp leading to the Lehigh Valley's passenger station. The New York State Barge Canal Terminal is seen in the distance on the left. At the right center is the dam used to control water for the Rochester Gas and Electric Company's hydroelectric station.

On a frosty February day in 1928, car No. 2008 boarded passengers bound for the city at the Winton Road Station. The stairway leading to the platform is on the right. Today, motorists speed along this corridor on I-490, few realizing that both the Erie Canal and the subway once used this route. (Courtesy of the Rochester chapter NRHS.)

This unusual photograph was taken on August 6, 1952, from the rear window of a subway car on its way downtown. Many Rochesterians would enjoy a ride if time could be turned back. Culver Road Station is seen in the distance at the right. (Wallace Bradley photograph, courtesy of the Rochester chapter NRHS.)

A pair of subway cars poses for a photograph near the Driving Park Avenue carbarn in 1942. The series 2000 cars were rebuilt with a center-entrance, center-exit design. Fares were collected by the conductor standing behind a curved white bar at the center of the car. (Courtesy of the Rochester chapter NRHS.)

This was a day full of nostalgia, as passengers boarded subway car No. 48. It was the last run on Rochester's $14 million subway. The traction era came to a close on Saturday, June 30, 1956, when motorman Harry A. Beach left City Hall Station and the subway car disappeared into the pages of history.

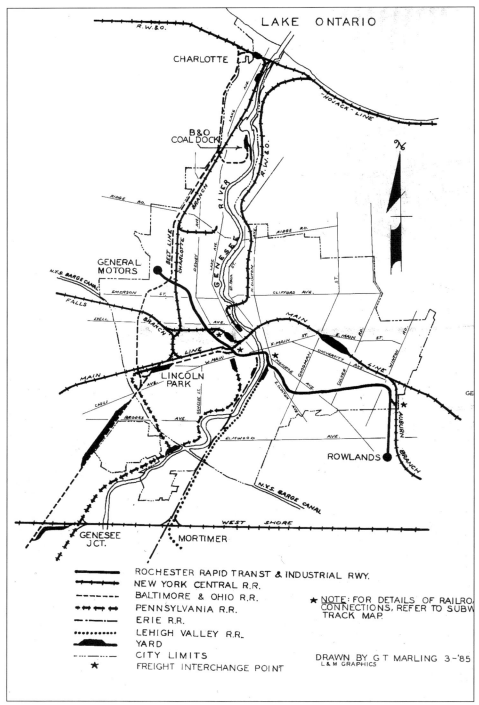

In 1985, G.T. Marling drew this revealing map that clearly depicts both the route of the subway from Rowlands to General Motors and the five major rail lines that transferred goods to and from the city during former years. (Courtesy of the Rochester chapter NRHS.)

98

Seven

AUTOMOBILES, TRUCKS, AND BUSES

At the dawn of the horseless carriage, this early traffic control was attempted in Rochester. Imagine the lonely gentleman shivering and muttering, "Haven't seen a dratted benzene burner, road machine in an hour. I just can't wait for someone to invent the traffic stop light."

How proud Sergeant Francis B. Allen appears sitting next to the driver. When Officer Allen retired at age 89 from the Rochester police force in 1926, he was the oldest policeman on active duty in the nation. This photograph, taken in 1907, displays the city's first motorized paddy wagon. Note the solid rubber tires and nifty chain drive.

The automobile age was in its infancy when the state was inspired to require autoists to pay for a driver's license and have road vehicles equipped with license plates. Naturally, it meant the opening of Rochester's first license bureau. There are three clerks just waiting for a customer. The low plate number on the open touring car is No. 868.

This unique advertisement appeared in the January 1904 issue of *Scientific American*. George B. Selden of Rochester is considered by most the "Father of the Automobile." In 1877, he was first in the nation to move a wagon powered by an internal combustion engine. He patented his road machine and received royalties from the automobile makers listed in this advertisement. He warned others that he would sue if they infringed on his patient. Henry Ford did and was sued.

Here is a look at one of Rochester's first van delivery trucks. Note the spoke wheels, distinctive horn, dropped windshield, and spare tire. There is even a handy crank below the radiator if the starter fails to work.

REGAS

Air-Cooled Automobile

Maximized Strength, Lightness, Speed, Safety, Style and Comfort, at a minimum of first cost and final expense. New and distinctly novel design. A light Tonneau Car with side entrance. A novelty in this country. Obviates dismounting in muddy roads. A model of perfection in design, mechanism, workmanship and material, this scientifically-constructed machine of 12 horse power at a speed of 1,200 revolutions per minute, moves with almost a complete elimination of vibration. The Regas is especially constructed to resist all kinds of strains, achieve a high percentage of mileage, and at the same time retain the distinct advantages of smooth running, ample convenience and ease of operation. Any ordinary ability is sufficient to master the details of this simple and luxurious car.

PRICE $ 1,500
REGAS AUTOMOBILE COMPANY
Rochester, New York

This 1904 advertisement in *Scientific American* is clear evidence that Rochester had one automobile maker that history has overlooked. The Regas air-cooled automobile sold for a cool $1,500. The Regas name may have derived from the reversal of the last names of J. Harry Sager or Charles Sager, who both operated automobile dealerships in Rochester.

ARRANGEMENT OF SLOTTED TUBES ON
REGAS CYLINDER.

Rochester boasted of its custom-made Cunningham cars, its Seldon autos and trucks, and even a vehicle run by steam, but has entirely overlooked the splendid, two-cylinder 1904 Regas. Note its innovative air-cooling system; its 12-horse-power engine that turned at 1,200 revolutions per minute with "almost a complete elimination of vibration;" and the handy side entrance that "obviates dismounting in muddy roads."

REGAS 12-HORSEPOWER CAR WITH SIDE ENTRANCE TONNEAU AND 4½ X 5
TWO-CYLINDER AIR-COOLED MOTOR.

The old convention center, now home to GeVa (Genesee Valley Players) Theatre, was the arena for Rochester's first automobile show. This 1908 photograph was taken from the balcony overlooking all of the snappy, new models. Several firms promoted their automobile-associated goods with displays in the balcony.

The main floor of the convention center was packed with dozens of the latest models: sedans, touring cars, tonneaus, and broughams. The shiny automobiles' profiles could be inspected, the engines examined, and all the latest accessories admired.

The past is filled with memories surrounding the automobile. Mr. and Mrs. Hadley and their daughter could not be prouder of their sturdy Paige touring car c. 1916.

Not everyone took the trolley to the park. Opening day at Eastman and Durand Park is recorded in this 1909 photograph. Scores have motored down to the new park. A gift of Dr. Henry Durand and George Eastman, the 965-acre park has 5,000 feet of Lake Ontario waterfront, an arboretum, and a public golf course. Its dedication was followed by a dramatized Native American battle and a game of lacrosse. Lakeshore Boulevard looks a little different today.

This uncommon photograph captures the fire department's almost-full transition from horse power to gasoline power. The department's main headquarters, at 37–67 Central Avenue, provides the background for the c. 1930 photograph of its motorized pumper, hook and ladder truck, and fire chief's car. Only the old water tower wagon is still moved by three horses.

Motorization of the fire department began May 1, 1912. That is when hose company No. 3 on Platt Street displayed both styles of fire apparatus. On the right, George Roeper holds the reins to Jack and Baldy, harnessed to their vintage hose wagon. On the left is a brand new Pope-Hartford combination chemical and hose truck that replaced the two horse-power wagon.

105

This pre-1929 view looks west toward the former Rochester city hall. The photograph shows the parking lot on the corner of Broad and Exchange Streets. The vintage cars all date prior to 1929. Note the wooden voting booths on the sidewalk adjacent to city hall.

The parking lot seen above became the site for the Genesee Valley Trust Company, which opened in 1931. The new building's "Wings of Progress" were designed by architect Ralph T. Walker. A subway entrance parallels the left side of the Times Square Building.

This *c.* 1919 photograph proves that in a match between an automobile and a train, the winner is not the automobile. Standing second from the right is Milton Wilcox, and standing third from the right is Ernest Haker. It is hard to believe that the pile of scrap metal was once an automobile.

It was a grim day for the driver of this automobile. This accident happened to the Gipaud car on April 8, 1937. A state trooper on the right is keeping the curious away from the road.

Like a giant hand, a hurricane-force wind twisted its way through the city's northwest neighborhoods on July 1, 1932. Cutting a half-mile wide swath of destruction, Rochester's only recorded tornado lasted less than 20 minutes. It caused thousands of dollars in damage and workmen spent weeks sawing up giant elm trees and clearing debris from Lyell, Lake, and Dewey Avenues. This photograph shows one of nine automobiles that were "bounced like rubber balls and demolished." In the Jones Park area, the storm sucked this car from its garage and crunched it into the owner's house.

The vintage Brockway truck looks like it has delivered its last shipment of Economy Reduction Soap. While the truck's frame was made of steel, much of the body seems to be fabricated with wood. The material made up the cab, the truck bed, and the sides. Note the battered toolbox on the running board.

The intersection of East Main and Goodman Streets appears in this 1940s photograph in a view looking west toward the bridge over the New York Central tracks. Plymouths, Chevrolets, Pontiacs, and a white Metro truck are part of this frozen moment in time. Gasoline and tires were rationed, and new automobiles were unavailable. Pedestrian traffic increased and public transportation blossomed. (Courtesy of the New York Museum of Transportation.)

The Equipment that lasts

One Rochester firm that capitalized on the growth of the automobile was the Rochester Coil Company, which was renamed the North East Electric Company in 1909. The company manufactured electric starters, horns, speedometers, and other automobile accessories. In 1929, the firm was purchased by the Dayton Electric Company and became Delco.

No Rochesterian who drove an early automobile became more famous than Blanche Stuart Scott. Born on Scott Road (now Mount Read Boulevard), the 13-year-old redhead drove her dad's car throughout the city (no law forbid it in 1899). By age 24, she convinced the Willys-Overland Motor Company that she could drive their automobile from New York City to San Francisco. With the motto "the car, the girl and the wide wide world" painted on the automobile, she crossed the nation, covering 5,393 miles and only 220 of them were paved. She was first women to do so. She was also the first American women to fly a plane, as well as the only Rochester native to have her image on a U.S. postage stamp. (Courtesy of the Glen H. Curtiss Museum.)

Another proud Rochester company connected with the automobile industry was Rochester Products, once a division of General Motors. This brochure cover illustrates its human dimensions.

Rochesterians working at the Rochester Products 400,000-square-foot plant were responsible for the manufacture of lighters, locks and keys, refrigeration units, miles of tubing, and at one time, 25,000 carburetors daily. In 1999, the Delphi Energy and Chassis Systems, a division of the Delphi Corporation, became the parent company.

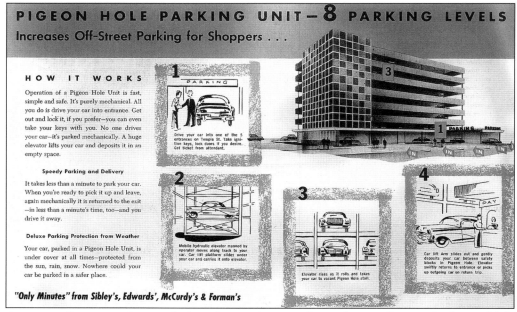

An extraordinary way the city dealt with its parking needs was the installation of a Pigeon Hole Parking Unit. This unique structure could hold 240 cars at a time on its eight levels.

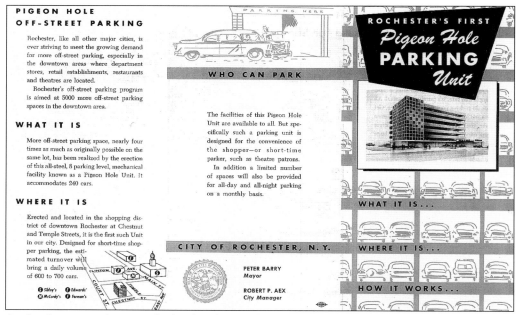

As the diagram indicates, a hydraulic elevator lifted cars and slotted them into "pigeon holes." This map shows that the entrance to the garage was on Temple Street, off Chestnut Street. The garage was dismantled and sold to Poughkeepsie, New York, when its site was purchased for the construction of Mid-Town Plaza.

Few of us may recall when Greyhound buses, c. 1930, had this appearance. The wonderful bit of nostalgia had to be included as another link in Rochester's transportation history.

The Megiddo Mission on Thurston Road once had a traveling band that delivered the gospel to villages and towns throughout the eastern United States. This rare photograph of the 13 musicians was snapped in the early 1920s. A window in their Brockway bus bears the admonition "Search the Scriptures."

On July 11, 1973, Mayor Stephen May is seen on the right holding street plans with councilman Charles Schiano on the left. Other city and county dignitaries look on. The much-widened roadway passing the former Bausch and Lomb complex was renamed Upper Falls Boulevard.

A major link in I-490 across the Genesee River was the Troop-Howell Street Bridge. The official ribbon-cutting ceremony took place on October 1, 1973. Pictured on the far left is Mayor May, and holding the ribbon on the right is Lucien Moran, the Monroe County manager. The view is looking east.

Eight

AIRPLANES AND AIRPORTS

Genesee Valley Park was filled with spectators on September 1, 1911, when John J. Frisbee, a noted balloonist, flew his rickety Curtiss plane from the Rochester Aero Club field. Powered with a two-cycle engine manufactured by Rochester's Elbridge Engine Company, his flight took him over Cobb's Hill, into the city and back. It was the first flight over downtown, and during the entire flight he was never more than 300 feet off the ground.

This faded image of Blanch Stuart Scott in the pilot's seat of Glen Curtiss's *June Bug* displays a remarkable woman associated with an even more remarkable feat. Scott was learning to fly, "cutting daisies" on the ground, when a wind gust lifted her into the air. On June 6, 1910, Scott became the first American woman to fly an airplane.

Crowds gathered at Crittenden Park in 1914 to witness the acrobatics of Rochester's aerial pioneer, Lincoln Beachey, who did not disappoint the air enthusiasts. He drove his biplane with its canvas wings and bamboo struts toward the grandstand, swooping up just yards from the structure and the startled spectators. He then steered his craft upward and performed the first aerial loop-the-loop ever seen in the Flower City.

Another chapter was added to Rochester's aviation history on July 29, 1927, when Charles Lindbergh landed his *Spirit of St. Louis* at Rochester's early airfield. Mayor Martin B. O'Neil was on hand to greet him, as were more than 25,000 Rochesterians. Lindbergh, who just completed his famous transatlantic flight in May, stopped here for an hour while en route to a Buffalo air show.

Associated with Charles Lindbergh was Trans World Airlines. Seen at the Rochester Municipal Airport, *c.* the 1930s, is one of the airline's latest airships, a DC-3.

This first-day cancellation was purchased for 25¢ by Lenard Babin, aerophilatelist, on August 17, 1930. The cancellation was part of the events marking the dedication of Rochester's new airport. An aerial circus was also sponsored by the American Legion to coincide with the dedication ceremonies.

A glance backward in time is offered through this 1930s postcard view of the Rochester Municipal Airport. The photograph reveals three hangers, an administrative addition, a searchlight beacon tower, and the airport control tower. The field was located on Scottsville Road.

SPONSORED BY THE AMERICAN LEGION

ROCHESTER AIR RACES

ROCHESTER AIRPORT   ROCHESTER, N. Y.

September 23-24, 1933

Under Management of American Air Aces, Inc.

Pre-Sale   Free Parking

40c   2   N⁰   **5578**

This ticket to the Rochester Air Races, held at Rochester's airport, was discovered in someone's scrapbook of memories. The 40¢ admission fare was sold by the American Legion for the air races the legion sponsored on September 23 and 24, 1933.

A young lad on a bicycle has stopped to watch the planes land and take off at the city's old airport. This 1939 photograph shows a line of cars, possibly holding other flying enthusiasts.

A brand-new airport replaced the Scottsville Road site with a formal opening and rededication on June 21, 1953. Both city and county officials were present to host guests at the airport's new location on Brooks Avenue. This brochure was provided to the guests.

This photograph shows the passenger terminal and administration building of what was known in 1953 as the Rochester-Monroe County Airport. A brick clock tower may have served to remind those departing from the air facility how much time they had to buy their tickets and board their planes.

Huge picture windows enabled visitors and passengers to view the planes as they landed and departed. A restaurant called Horizons offered fine dining to the public and passengers awaiting their flights.

Beyond the windows, an acre or more of concrete permitted planes to taxi up to the terminal. Passengers had a little fresh air while walking to their plane. An observation platform was located on the roof, as seen in the left center of the photograph.

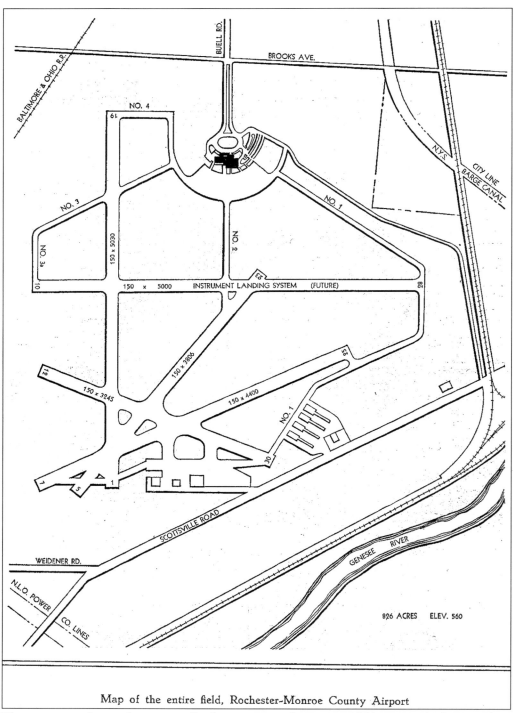

Map of the entire field, Rochester-Monroe County Airport

This map was designed to orient Rochesterians to their new, 1953 airport facilities and its runways. Note that railroad tracks, the canal, and surrounding roads limited the runway length. At the time, several gasoline and oil-tank farms were a hazard at the airport's southeast approach.

Nine

PRESERVING OUR TRANSPORTATION HERITAGE

The Ebert boys, Morgan and Jonas, were lucky enough to have a ride in the cab of one of the diesel locomotives of the Rochester chapter of the National Railway Historical Society. The occasion for the smiling visitors was the chapter's annual Diesel Days, or picnic. The chapter is a partner with the New York Museum of Transportation on East River Road, joined to preserve our area's transportation legacy for today's visitors and for generations to come.

In 1853, the Rochester and Genesee Valley Railroad operated between Avon and Rochester. By 1909, the Erie Railroad purchased the route and erected a new depot, seen here, at what is now Industry, New York. The Erie added a catenary line between Mount Morris and Rochester that operated an electric-powered combination passenger and freight car from 1907 to 1934.

The Erie depot on Route 251 in Rush, New York, was abandoned and became a target for vandals and the ravages of time. The Rochester chapter of the National Railway Historical Society purchased the structure in 1979, restoring and transforming it into a vintage rail museum. A sizable collection of early rail cars and diesel and steam locomotives was added to the complex that operates over a two-mile railroad built by chapter members. (Courtesy of Gene Davis.)

The interior of the station master's office in the depot has been returned to the appearance it once had in the 1920s. Telegraph equipment, lanterns, a pot-bellied stove, and an order-board lever stand help visitors to recall the days when steam engines made daily stops at the depot. (Courtesy of Gene Davis.)

The folks at the New York Museum of Transportation, at 6393 East River Road, have beautifully restored the Rochester & Eastern Railroad trolley No. 157. Retired from city streets, it became Father Edelman's camp on Irondequoit Bay. Later, hauled to the Magee Museum in Pennsylvania, it suffered in a flood. Returned to Rochester in 1975, it has been reborn, becoming a transportation prize from the past. (Courtesy of Gene Davis.)

The New York Transportation Museum presents many educational displays. Dick Langkamp inspects two 19th-century handcars used to transfer track crews from place to place. Exhibits include trolley cars, early carriages, trucks, buses, and other transportation-related vehicles. A sizable model-train layout attracts kids of all ages. (Courtesy of Gene Davis.)

Neil Bellenger assists John Redden, who is working in the smoke box, helping to refurbish the 1918 Vulcan saddle-tank steam engine No. 12 at the Rochester chapter of the National Railway Historical Society restoration facility. The 0-4-0 locomotive is one of two steam engines the chapter is currently restoring.

James Dierks, one of the directors at the New York Museum of Transportation, has recently acquired two operable trolleys for the museum. He is making minor repairs in preparation for rides by visitors. Overhead, catenary wire for the trolley's propulsion can be seen in the background. On occasion, the public is invited to ride the trolley, a nostalgic experience missing from the area for almost 50 years.

The two transportation museums are fortunate to have Charles Robinson, a writer, trolley enthusiast, and competent motorman and conductor, as a member. Here, he is awaiting the public to board trolley No. 168 on its maiden run in 2001 over the museum's loop track.

Engineer Eugene Redden, on the left, is joined by rail-fan John Ebert for a memorable ride in the cab of a superbly restored locomotive that once served the Nickel Plate Road. The locomotive is one of seven diesel engines the chapter has restored for museum operation.

Three open-sided track cars are available to shuttle visitors on a two-mile, scenic excursion between the New York Museum of Transportation and the Rochester and Genesee Valley Depot Museum during the warm-weather months. (Courtesy of Gene Davis.)